W9-ATD-847

A Note to Parents

DK READERS is a compelling program for beginning readers, designed in conjunction with leading literacy experts, including Dr. Linda Gambrell, Director of the Eugenge T. Moore School of Education at Clemson University. Dr. Gambrell has served on the Board of Directors of the International Reading Association and as President of the National Reading Conference.

Beautiful illustrations and superb full-color photographs combine with engaging, easy-to-read stories to offer a fresh approach to each subject in the series. Each DK READER is guaranteed to capture a child's interest while developing his or her reading skills, general knowledge, and love of reading.

The five levels of DK READERS are aimed at different reading abilities, enabling you to choose the books that are exactly right for your child:

Pre-level 1 – Learning to read
Level 1   – Beginning to read
Level 2   – Beginning to read alone
Level 3   – Reading alone
Level 4   – Proficient readers

The "normal" age at which a child begins to read can be anywhere from three to eight years old, so these levels are only a general guideline.

No matter which level you select, you can be sure that you are helping your child learn to read, then read to learn!

DK

LONDON, NEW YORK, MUNICH,
MELBOURNE, AND DELHI

Series Editor Deborah Lock
Senior Art Editor Tory Gordon-Harris
U.S. Editor Elizabeth Hester
Design Assistant Sadie Thomas
Production Claire Pearson
DTP Designer Almudena Díaz

Reading Consultant
Linda Gambrell, Ph.D.

First American Edition, 2003
03 04 05 06 07 10 9 8 7 6 5 4 3 2 1
Published in the United States by DK Publishing, Inc.
375 Hudson Street, New York, New York 10014

Published in Great Britain by Dorling Kindersley Limited.

Library of Congress Cataloging-in-Publication Data
Colorful day / Linda Gambrell, consultant.
p. cm. -- (Dk readers)
Summary: Explores a variety of colors seen in the different seasons from
winter through spring and summer to fall.
ISBN 0-7894-9799-9 (pbk.) -- ISBN 0-7894-9798-0 (plc)
[1. Color--Fiction. 2. Seasons--Fiction.] I. Title. II. Series:
Dorling Kindersley readers.
PZ7.C71638 2003
[E]--dc21
2003004139

Color reproduction by Colourscan, Singapore
Printed and bound in China by L Rex Printing Co., Ltd.

The publisher would like to thank the following for
their kind permission to reproduce their photographs:
a=above; c=center; b=below; l=left; r=right t=top;

British Museum: 28br, 32br; **Corbis:** Bill Ross 8cl; Craig Tuttle 21br;
Jeremy Horner 4c; **Gables Travels:** 16-17; **Getty Images:** Jerry Driendl 10-
11; Darrell Gulin 8-9; Terry Husebye 26-27; Tom King 15tr; Mike Timo 6-
7; **Paul Goff:** 27bl; **Judith Miller & Dorling Kindersley & Bonhams,
Edinburgh:** 13bl; **Tracy Morgan:** 2crb, 8bl; **Natural History Museum:**
9bcr, 19bcl, 19bcl, 25br; **Stephen Oliver:** 2tr, 11bc, 12bc, 12br, 15bc, 18-
19, 19br, 26bl, 32c; **Guy Ryecart:** 17bc; Ross Simms and the Winchcombe
Folk & Police Museum: 2cra, 22bl; **Barrie Watts:** 2br, 7br;
Jerry Young: 22-23, 24-25, 25c, 32bl;

All other images © Dorling Kindersley.
For further imformation see: www.dkimages.com

Discover more at
www.dk.com

LEARNING pre-level **1** TO READ

Colorful Days

DK

DK Publishing, Inc.

How many colors

green

yellow

pink

red

Come and
play with me.

can you see?

nose

mouth

white

~eye

We can play
in the cold,
white snow.

We can look at
the purple flowers.

leaf

purple

8

petal

blossom

We can run
around the
trees with the
pink blossoms.

pink

petal

eye ————

gray

ear

fur

We can pet
the small,
gray rabbits.

We can sail with
the boats on the
blue water.

mast

sail

blue

deck

We can walk
through the
tall, yellow
sunflowers.

yellow

seeds

petal

orange

We can eat
a cold, orange
ice pop.

ice pop

stick

boots

red

We can kick the
leaves and pick
the red apples.

tree

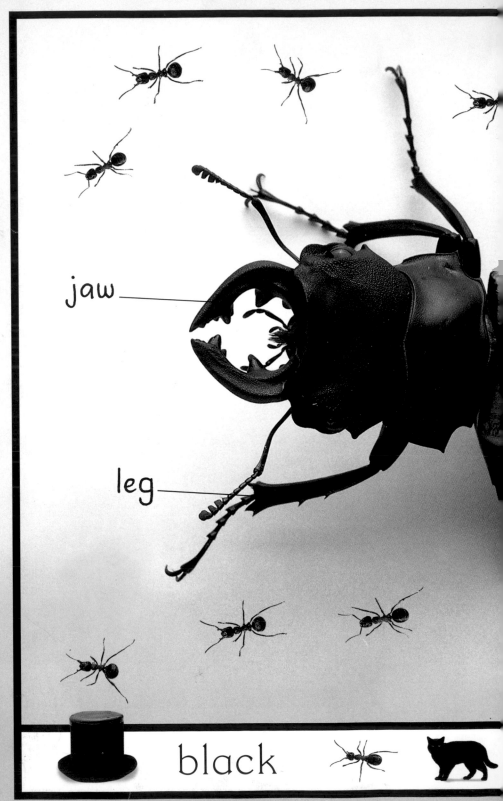

jaw

leg

black

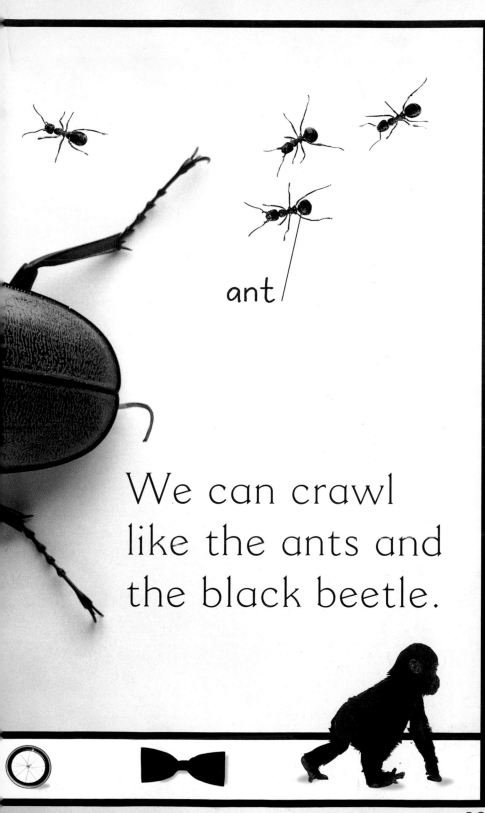

ant

We can crawl
like the ants and
the black beetle.

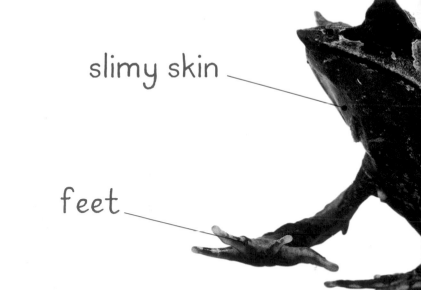

slimy skin

feet

brown

We can croak
like the small,
brown frogs.

branches

needles

 green

We can run around
the tall, green trees.

We can hang
silver balls and
put on gold crowns.

silver

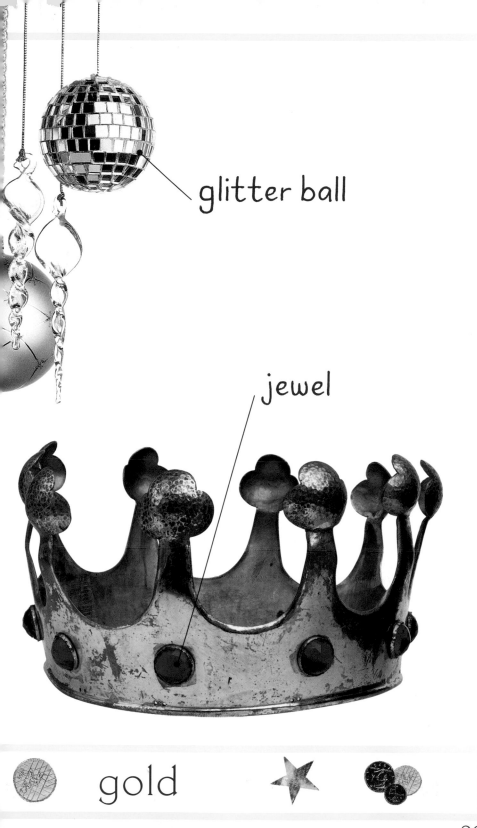

glitter ball

jewel

gold

How many colors

can you see?

Picture word list

white
page 6

purple
page 8

pink
page 10

gray
page 12

blue
page 14

yellow
page 16

orange
page 18

red
page 20

black
page 22

brown
page 24

green
page 26

silver and **gold**
page 28